WHSmith

Practice

English

Ron Simpson

Contents

Introduction	2
Forming sentences: subject and verb	3
Direct and indirect objects	5
Complements	7
How to use adverbs	9
Joining sentences: compounds	11
Complex sentences	13
Full stops	15
More about full stops	17
Question marks and exclamation marks	19
Colons and semicolons	21
Activities	23
More about colons	27
Commas	29
More about commas	31
Dashes, hyphens and brackets	33
Apostrophes	35
Punctuating speech	37
More about speech punctuation	39
Summarising punctuation	41
Paragraphing	43
Answers	45

**Age 12–14
Years 8–9
Key Stage 3**

Introduction

How to do well in English

There are many aspects of English that are not covered by rules or judged by how well you do exercises. Imagination and reasoning power are as important as writing correctly. You can only improve your vocabulary by reading widely, learning new words and trying them out. However, it is important that underlying all of those things is a correct use of language. If you write correctly and unimaginatively, the result is boring. If you write with imagination but no control, the result is as bad, but confusing rather than boring!

How to use English *Practice*

Before you start, you will need an exercise book of your own for copying and completing the exercises. As you work through the books, when you are confident you have answered all the questions in an exercise correctly, move on. If you feel you need more practice, follow a different explanation where possible or re-read the relevant section. On *Try it Yourself!* pages, unless told otherwise, you should do the activity before reading the notes at the side. Finally the middle four pages of each book contain activities for which you will need to cut up the pages. For this reason you need to photocopy these pages and put the pieces somewhere safe so you can use them again.

Every effort has been made to trace all copyright holders, but if any have been inadvertently overlooked the Publishers will be pleased to make the necessary arrangements at the first opportunity.

Hachette UK's policy is to use papers that are natural, renewable and recyclable products and made from wood grown in sustainable forests. The logging and manufacturing processes are expected to conform to the environmental regulations of the country of origin.

Orders: please contact Bookpoint Ltd, 130 Milton Park, Abingdon, Oxon OX14 4SB. Telephone: (44) 01235 827720. Fax: (44) 01235 400454. Lines are open 9.00a.m.–5.00p.m., Monday to Saturday, with a 24-hour message answering service. Visit our website at www.hoddereducation. co.uk.

© Ron Simpson 2013
Teacher's tips © David Belsey 2013
First published in 2007 exclusively for WHSmith by
Hodder Education
An Hachette UK Company
338 Euston Road
London NW1 3BH

This second edition first published in 2013 exclusively for WHSmith by Hodder Education.

Impression number   10 9 8 7 6 5 4 3 2 1
Year   2018 2017 2016 2015 2014 2013

All rights reserved. Apart from any use permitted under UK copyright law, no part of this publication may be reproduced or transmitted in any form or by any means, electronic or mechanical, including photocopying and recording, or held within any information storage and retrieval system, without permission in writing from the publisher or under licence from the Copyright Licensing Agency Limited. Further details of such licences (for reprographic reproduction) may be obtained from the Copyright Licensing Agency Limited, Saffron House, 6–10 Kirby Street, London EC1N 8TS.

Cover illustration by Oxford Designers and Illustrators Ltd
All other illustrations by Fakenham Prepress Solutions, Fakenham, Norfolk NR21 8NN
Typeset in 16pt Folio by Fakenham Prepress Solutions, Fakenham, Norfolk NR21 8NN
Printed in Italy

A catalogue record for this title is available from the British Library.

ISBN: 978 1444 189 285

Forming sentences: subject and verb

Get started

How do the main parts of speech fit together to make a sentence?

The shortest sentence consists simply of a **subject** (a **noun** or **pronoun**) and a **verb**.

The finger beckoned. **Night fell.**
Tom was running. **My mother laughed.**
I lost.

These are all very short, but they *are* sentences because they make sense on their own.

Practice

- A verb can be one word or two or more (such as *was running*).
- A verb relates to a particular time, and so is in a certain **tense**.
- A verb must be capable of following a subject. This means that some parts of the verb (like **participles**) are not suitable. *Running* can refer to different times (*is running*, *was running*, *will be running*) and does not make sense after a subject (*I running*, *Mr McAvoy running*) – unless with another verb (*Mr McAvoy was running*).
- A subject can be a single-word noun or pronoun or a single noun with a definite or indefinite article (*the car*, *an accident*, *a fire*).
- A subject can also be a noun with an adjective or adjectives added before or, less often, after (*The long, black car …* or *A fire, warm and cosy, …*).
- A subject can be a phrase which has no single main noun in it, but which does the job of a noun. Look at this example: **How to stop losing money was the main point of discussion.** If you put the adjectives and noun *Our financial loss* as the subject, it would make similar sense. So *How to stop losing money* is a **noun phrase**, doing the job of a noun as subject of the sentence.

The principle is easy: there might be all sorts of extra bits added on, but the simplest sentence is basically just **subject**/**verb**.

A question of sentences

This section concentrates on sentences that are **statements**.

Do not forget that sentences can be **questions** and **commands** too.

In many ways, questions and commands are the same as statements, but, apart from things like question marks, there is one important difference in each case:

- **Questions** – Often a verb is divided up in a question. A statement may say, **I had a good time on holiday.** For a question, *had* is divided into *did have*: **Did you have a good time on holiday?**
- **Commands** – These are the only full sentences without subjects. If you are giving an order, there is no need to say who is doing the action. It is obvious – it is the person you are talking to. A statement says, **Carl had to tidy his bedroom before going out.** The command Carl received was **Tidy your bedroom before you go out.**

3

Verbs: complete and incomplete

Some verbs are complete in themselves:

All my friends came.

In winter the ice froze.

The wind howled and the thunder rumbled.

But many verbs need something added to make sense:

My mother caught ...

Caught what? The bus, a cold or you misbehaving?

Our class was told to bring ...

Bring what? Homework, nature specimens or money for the class trip?

Think what verbs like *catch* and *bring* need to complete a sentence.

Now see the next page.

Try it yourself!

Find the sentences

Remember:
- All sentences except commands have a subject (a noun or word/s doing the job of a noun) and a verb which relates to a time (e.g. past tense).
- Commands do not need a subject.

In the examples that follow, some are sentences, some are not. Copy them all into your exercise book. Then, after each one, indicate **statement** (S), **question** (Q), **command** (C) or **not a sentence** (NS). If you think it is a sentence, mark the **subject** and the **verb** by underlining or ringing.

Some of the subjects and verbs consist of more than one word, so mark both or all the words. There are other parts to the sentences – just ignore these.

Sangeeta and Kate went to the same school.
Outside the cinema.
Buying an ice cream from the supermarket.
I will see you tomorrow.
Did the boy bring the right paper?
How could the referee see from there?
A pint of milk, please.
Pass me the milk, please.
Digging the garden tired me out.
Say good morning to Mr Howells.
I want you to meet Mr Howells.
Mr Howells to see you.
Why did you wake me so early?
Half past seven.
To get all the answers right is difficult.

Check your answers on **pages 45–48**.

All correct?

If so, congratulations. One or two of those were very difficult.

Do not worry if you missed those long phrases as subjects. However, if you made any mistakes about which were sentences, compare your answers to the definition of what makes a sentence at the top of this page.

Teacher's tips

Practise turning statements into questions or commands e.g. *It is important to write in sentences. Is it important to write in sentences? Write in sentences! It is important.* Notice how the word order sometimes has to change.

4

Direct and indirect objects

Get started

Some actions are complete in themselves; some are complete only if there is a person or thing for the action to be done to.

This 'done to' part of the sentence is called the **direct object**:

I handed my book in.
The production toured the country.
My mother bought a bright red car.
I knew what to expect.

It is fairly straightforward, except for that awkward phrase in the last sentence. Remember that the sentence could be I knew the answer, with *answer* doing just the same job as *what to expect*.

Practice

What is the object in this sentence?

I gave the teacher my book.

Who or what is on the end of the giving: the teacher or the book?
In fact, both are the objects of the sentence:

- The **direct object** has the action done directly to it/him/her/them. In this case, *my book* was lifted up and passed from hand to hand.
- If someone/something receives the direct object, he/she/it is called the **indirect object**.

A good way to identify an indirect object is to remember that, if the direct object goes first, the indirect object follows the word *to*.

Does it make sense to write: I gave my book to the teacher? Yes.

Does it make sense to write: I gave the teacher to my book? Not really.

Therefore *book* is the direct object and *teacher* the indirect object.

Remember, though, that *to* is not necessary if the indirect object goes first.

Verbs: complete and incomplete (continued)

Some verbs need a direct object to complete the action. *He ran* makes sense, but *he threw* inspires the question *what*?
However, verbs do not divide simply into those that have an object and those that do not. Many verbs can do either:

When he was feeling energetic, he ran to school.
Our neighbours ran a shop.

In the second example, *ran* has an object: *shop*.

And there are plenty more:

He tried hard.
He tried a piece of my cake.

I sat in the train.
My father sat me down and explained the problem., etc., etc., etc.

What are these verbs called?

A verb which needs an object is called a **transitive verb** and one that cannot have an object is **intransitive**.
As mentioned above, many verbs can be either transitive or intransitive.

A first word about prepositions

Prepositions are often very short, but they are very important in making sentences work. A preposition is placed before a noun or pronoun to join it to the rest of the sentence. So far, we have met *to* which can be used to link an indirect object to the rest of a sentence.

You can probably think of other uses *to* has.

Can you think of some other prepositions?

Words and phrases

Noun phrases were mentioned on page 23.

A phrase is a group of words, but not a full sentence.

These groups of words do the job of a particular part of speech, so there are also **adjective phrases** and **adverb phrases**.

For example, you could describe a man by writing *the strong man*, using an adjective. If you wrote *the man with muscles like iron*, that would be an adjective phrase.

Try it yourself!

Put them together

Turn to the activity on **page 23**.

You will see a page full of nouns, pronouns, noun phrases and verbs.

Your task is to put them together in as many sentences as you can, all consisting of subject – verb – direct object, or subject – verb – indirect object – direct object.

Write the sentences in your exercise book and try to find as many cases as you can:

- where you can reverse the sentence, turning subject into object and object into subject
- where there are all four parts: subject, verb, direct object and indirect object.

Compare your answers to the suggestions on **pages 45–48**.

Watch out for pronouns

Pronouns take a different form depending on whether they are subject or object:

She took **me** to the park.   **I** took **her** to the park.

Copy the following sentences into your exercise book, writing out the correct pronoun as you go:

The taxi collected (they/them) at the airport.
Joanna's aunt sent (she/her) a birthday card.
Jack and (I/me) were playing by the river.
The invitation was addressed to my brother and (I/me).
(She/her) expected (I/me) to help (she/her) with her homework.

Check your answers on **pages 45–48**.

All correct?

Most were very easy, but some people have a problem when *I* or *me* follows a noun and *and*. The rule is quite simple: use the same pronoun as if the noun was not there. **The invitation was addressed to I** is obviously wrong, so do not write **The invitation was addressed to my brother and I.**

Teacher's tips

Remember that writers make choices. Sentences can often be arranged in different ways for different effects e.g. *I read the book with enthusiasm. Enthusiastically, I read the book. I read the book, enthused. I enthusiastically read the book.* Where you place objects and phrases affects how the reader feels.

Complements

Get started

Though it is possible to imagine a situation where *I am!* becomes a full statement, generally verbs of being need something else to complete their meaning:

Maya became   **Natasha seems**   **Mr Brown was**

These subject/verb combinations do not mean anything.

But what can be added to a verb of being? Not an object because that is 'done to' by the verb and a verb of being cannot *do* anything.

What is needed is a **complement**.

Practice

A complement is something that *completes*.

	Subject	Verb	Complement
Noun complements	That man	was	my father.
	The school	became	a youth centre.

- The complement is equivalent to the subject, the same person or thing.

Adjective complements	That man	is	very tall.
	The school	seemed	empty.

- The complement says something about the subject.

Adverb complements	That man	was	on the plane.
	The school	is	behind the bus station.

Do not worry if you cannot tell the difference between noun, adjective and adverb complements: the exercises overleaf will help you with that. Just make sure that you are confident with these common forms of sentences:

subject – verb of doing – (indirect object) – direct object

subject – verb of being – complement

More prepositions

There are two prepositions in the table about complements: *on* and *behind*.

Prepositions are often used in adverb phrases to make the link with the rest of the sentence, and that link is important in showing the meaning. Just look at this obvious example:

in
under
My pen was behind the desk.
on
near

The prepositions do not just join *the desk* to the rest of the sentence. They also tell the reader how it fits in with everything else.

To be really correct...

Complements refer back to the subject; noun complements are essentially the same as the subject. So, if a pronoun is used for the noun complement, it really should be in the subject form:

It is I is strictly correct, not **It's me**.

In formal writing, stick to the rules. However, there are cases where it would just sound odd.

Not so simple

The structure of a sentence can sound very simple. When faced with a sentence on a page, however, it can be much more difficult to see the structure clearly. This is often because long phrases can do the job of subject, object or complement. Nouns might be surrounded by adjectives or adjective phrases.

Take the simple sentence:

The problem was difficult.

Enlarge or replace subject and complement with complicated phrases:

The most urgent problem before the committee was a consideration of the losses sustained at last year's event.

It is still the same structure: subject – verb – complement.

Wait and see

Adverbs are not always used as complements. The other parts they can play in a sentence can make simple sentences more complicated. Do not worry: the next section deals with adverbs.

Try it yourself!

Choose your complement

In the following sentences, there is a subject followed by a verb of being. Copy each sentence into your exercise book and complete it by adding a complement of the type stated, choosing from the list below:

Mrs Ackroyd became _____. (noun complement)
Mrs Ackroyd became _____. (adjective complement)
His walking stick was _____. (noun complement)
His walking stick was _____. (adjective complement)
His walking stick was _____. (adverb complement)
Hannah seemed _____. (adjective complement)
The holiday in Greece was _____. (adverb complement)
The holiday in Greece was _____. (adjective complement)
The holiday in Greece was _____. (noun complement)
Yesterday's news has become _____. (adjective complement)
Brazil became _____. (noun complement)
Brazil appeared _____. (adjective complement)
Brazil was _____. (adverb complement)
London is _____. (noun complement)
London is _____. (adverb complement)
London is _____. (adjective complement)

> **head of the company   in England's group   in the brochure
> expensive   extremely agitated   made of oak   happy
> my first choice   the capital city   world champions   in the hall
> unbeatable   his proudest possession   boring   in the South
> very busy**

Check your answers on **pages 45–48**.

All correct?

Just check that you understand this by creating another ending for each of the sentences above and writing these in your exercise book. You could begin:

> **Mrs Ackroyd became the county librarian.** (noun complement)
> **Mrs Ackroyd became worried about funding.** (adjective complement)
> … and so on. See how well you can do.

Teacher's tips

When you look over your written work, you will often find you have used complements. Try to vary what you have used. Have a mixture of noun, adjective and adverb complements. Vary your writing for the reader.

How to use adverbs

Get started

You can use an **adverb** or **adverb phrase** in any sentence. All sentences contain **verbs**, so there is every chance the writer might want to say more about the verb. Anything that gives more information about the verb is an adverb or (very often) an adverb phrase.

Practice

Look at this sentence. It takes the simplest subject – verb – direct object form:

The cinema shows films.

It makes sense, but it does not really say anything.

Add some bits to the nouns: an adjective (*new*), an adjective phrase (*in the shopping centre*) and a noun used as an adjective (*horror*):

The new cinema in the shopping centre shows horror films.

This is better, but there is a need for still more information. That is where adverbs come in. Mostly, adverbs and adverb phrases answer questions like: *When? Where? How? Why?*

As a matter of policy, the new cinema in the shopping centre regularly shows horror films on Friday afternoons in Screen Two.

Do the same thing for a typical subject – verb – complement sentence:

Rafik became terrified.

It makes sense, but it is short and unhelpful. Add the adverbs and adverb phrases:

At the fair, Rafik quickly became terrified of the ghost train.

Imagine the subject – verb – complement or subject – verb – object structure as being like a skeleton, a framework. If you want to build on it, there is plenty you can add, but you need to be aware of the skeleton underneath. Sometimes adding adverbs and adverb phrases is essential: in the example above, you would not know when to go to see the horror films without them. At other times, these extra details can add interest – so long as they are not overdone.

Adverb phrases

Remember that an adverb phrase does not have to include an adverb, just as noun phrases and adjective phrases do not always include nouns or adjectives. It simply has to do the *job* of an adverb.

I'll do the shopping soon.

Soon is an adverb. Now look at the following sentence:

I'll do the shopping in ten minutes.

In ten minutes consists of a preposition, an adjective and a noun, but it is serving as an adverb, so it is an adverb phrase.

Other jobs for adverbs

Adverbs are also used:
- with **adjectives** – To say more about an adjective, use an adverb: *very* unpleasant, *hopelessly* inefficient, *seriously* ill.
- with **adverbs** – The same as with adjectives: *painfully* slowly, *fairly* capably.

Here are some examples:

The quietly confident contestant smiled calmly.

This sentence contains two adverbs: one describes how he *smiled* (verb), the other how *confident* (adjective) he was. It would also have made sense to use the phrase *calmly confident contestant*. In this example, *calmly* relates to the adjective.

It hurt dreadfully.

It happened dreadfully quickly.

Here the same adverb is used in both sentences: in one case it tells about a verb (*hurt*), in the other it tells about an adverb (*quickly*).

9

Adverbs and whole sentences

You may be confused sometimes by finding what is obviously an adverb, but with no verb, adjective or adverb to relate to. *Oddly*, adverbs sometimes relate to the whole sentence. (And the sentence you have just read is an example of this!)

Again, examples are the easiest way to make this clear. Look at the word *clearly* (an adverb) in these two sentences:

Julia wrote very clearly.

This is normal adverbial use: the adverb describes the verb *wrote* – everyone could read her writing.

Clearly Julia had written to the police.

This says nothing about what her writing was like or whether it was easy to read. Instead, *clearly* suggests there is evidence that Julia had made contact with the police. In other words, it says that the whole sentence must have happened.

It is the same idea here:

Surprisingly I did well in the test.
Obviously I must be intelligent.

Try it yourself!

Mixing the sentences

Covering the main parts of what is called a **simple sentence** has proved that it is not always so simple. The pattern is something like this:

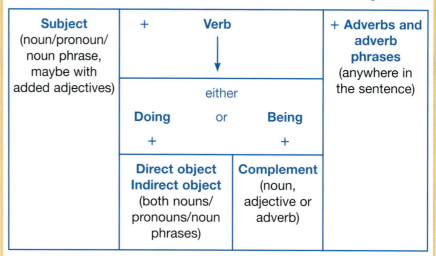

The activity you are going to do consists of taking all these elements and creating as many (long!) sentences as you can.

Turn to the activity on **page 24**.

Follow the instructions there, then write out a sentence in your exercise book:

- with a verb of being and complement
- with a verb of doing and direct and indirect objects
- as the first sentence above, but with at least one adverb or adverb phrase
- as the second sentence above, but with at least one adverb or adverb phrase
- as long as you can build that still makes sense.

Compare your answers to the suggestions on **pages 45–48**.

Are you happy with your answers?

Making the longest sentence you can is a useful way of showing how sentences work – and it can be fun.

But it is not the way to write well! In your own writing, make sure you have a good balance of short and long sentences, and avoid rambling and *confused* sentences.

Teacher's tips

Good writers use adverbs and adverb phrases in different places in a sentence to affect the reader e.g. *Slowly walking, he got tired. He got tired walking slowly. Slowly, he got tired walking.* You will need to think about using the comma to indicate emphasis and meaning.

Joining sentences: compounds

Get started

All the sentences dealt with so far have been **simple sentences**. Some of them may have seemed complicated, but they all have one thing in common:

They include only one verb with a subject and refer to a set time.

Sometimes you want to use more than one such verb.

In that case, you need to use a word that joins together two sentences. You may have come across various names for these words: *joining word*, *connective*, *connecting word*, and – the one used here – **conjunction**. If you think of the meanings of *join*, *junction* and *connect*, you will easily see what these words do.

Practice

Before going on, read the note **What is a clause?** on the right.

The simplest way of joining clauses is to join two **equal clauses** with a conjunction which gives no suggestion of which half is more important. The main conjunctions of this sort are:

- *but*: the two clauses contradict each other
- *so*: the first clause is a reason for the second
- *or*: the two clauses are alternatives
- *and*: the most common conjunction, which says absolutely nothing about the clauses except that they are joined together.

Making compound sentences is quite easy. Using them effectively is a little more difficult.

- A very common error is to simply write clause after clause with commas between them and no conjunctions. This is simply wrong (but see **An exception** overleaf).
- Something that is not wrong, but makes writing boring and tedious to read, is using *and* constantly. Try for some variety; the next section will deal with many more conjunctions.

What is a clause?

Put simply, a **clause** is something that is, or could have been, a sentence. A clause is a group of words with the crucial subject – verb combination.

So *going to the supermarket* is not a clause, but *I am going to the supermarket* is.

A **simple sentence** consists of one main clause.

A **compound sentence** (dealt with here) consists of two or more main clauses (sometimes called **coordinate clauses**).

A **complex sentence** (dealt with on pages 13–14) consists of a main clause and one or more less important clauses – known as **subordinate clauses**.

Are the names important?

It is important to know a suitable term for these joining words – either **conjunctions** or **connectives**.

It is less important (but can be interesting) to know that the sorts of conjunctions described in this section are called **coordinating conjunctions** and the ones in the next section are **subordinating conjunctions**.

A little extra meaning

Sometimes the conjunction you use can tell the reader a little bit extra. This is much more the case with complex sentences (see page 13), but it does happen with compound sentences.

Look at the following example:

The party was at Becky's so I decided to go.

The party was at Becky's, but I decided to go.

What does the choice of conjunction say about the speaker's feelings towards Becky?

An exception

Usually it is not correct to separate clauses by commas with no conjunctions. With more than two clauses, however, it is correct to save and until before the last one, just like in a list: ... salt, pepper, brown sauce and vinegar.

So it is wrong to say: Ashok went into the shop, he bought a chocolate bar.

But this is fine: Ashok went into the shop, bought a chocolate bar and paid for it out of his pocket money.

Try it yourself!

Forming compound sentences

Put a conjunction in the middle of the following pairs of simple sentences (and one group of three) and write out the full sentences in your exercise book. Decide which is the best conjunction; do not just put and every time.

The bell sounded ... the teacher continued with the lesson.

The bell sounded ... the teacher told the class to stop work.

The bell sounded ... the lights flashed.

The bell sounded ... the lights flashed ... the gates closed.

Did I hear the bell ... was that somebody's mobile phone?

It was Sunday ... I decided to stay in bed.

I thought I knew the way ... I took the wrong path through the woods.

I'll take a map next time ... I might get lost again.

Check your answers on pages 45–48. All correct?

If not, make sure that you know what your mistake was, then move on to something a bit more difficult.

Is there something shorter?

The simplest way to join two or more sentences is to connect them up with a conjunction and make no other change except removing a capital letter.

There are other ways, for instance, cutting down the number of clauses by getting rid of one of the subject – verb units.

For example: I hurried to catch the bus. I bumped into an old lady.

Turn the first verb into a participle: Hurrying to catch the bus, I bumped into an old lady.

... or get rid of it altogether: In my hurry to catch the bus, I bumped into an old lady.

What would you do with these?

The new hospital has more beds. It will serve the community more successfully.

You can buy groceries at the new supermarket. They are much cheaper.

My mother checked her mirrors. She pulled out into the traffic.

Compare your answers with those on pages 45–48.

Teacher's tips

Conjunctions can change and shape meaning. Consider how these words affect meaning in a sentence: *and, but, though, if, unless, because, then, despite, however, nevertheless, notwithstanding, although, though, conversely.*

Complex sentences

Get started

To create a **complex sentence** you need to:
- decide what is the most important clause
- decide how any other clauses fit in with it
- choose your **conjunction** to show that connection.

Suppose you had a music lesson on Saturday morning, then in the afternoon you went shopping. Which is the more important? That depends on the story you are telling:

> <u>Before</u> I went shopping, I had my music lesson. Mrs Blake gave me a new piece to practise.
> <u>After</u> I had my music lesson, I went shopping. I bought a new CD and some books.

What is the reason for the choice of main clause each time? The first story goes on to tell about the music lesson, so that is the main interest. The second one tells of your shopping trip, so the sentence is the other way round.

The connection made here (obviously enough) is of *time*.

Practice

Some of the connections conjunctions can make between main and subordinate clauses are of:

Time	when, before, after, whenever, while, as, since, until
Place	where
Reason	because, as, since (*note* – some conjunctions have two meanings)
Possibility	if, unless
Contrast	though, although

The first job of a conjunction or connective is (just like the names say) to join or to connect.

But connections can be made for different reasons, in different places.

Start with the statement **I was really happy last Saturday.**

What sort of connection makes sense?

- Time? <u>When</u> I got my new bike, ...
- Reason? ... <u>because</u> my tickets for the concert arrived.
- Or perhaps mentioning something less happy? ... <u>although</u> I'm not looking forward to going back to school.

Joined from a distance

As subordinating conjunctions join clauses together, it might seem to make sense for them to come in the middle, between the clauses. In fact, they are placed at the *beginning of the subordinate clause*, so, if that comes first, the conjunction is at the beginning of the sentence.

> I took the book off the shelf <u>and</u> I found the cover was torn.

But   <u>When</u> I took the book off the shelf, I found the cover was torn.

Another difficult term

It is important to use conjunctions accurately, but it is also interesting to know the correct term for the conjunctions in this section.

A *subordinate* is someone or something in a lower position, so the less important clauses are **subordinate clauses** and words like *although*, *when* and *because* are **subordinating conjunctions**.

How does this affect my writing?

The way you write in stories and other compositions can be improved by knowledge of different forms of sentences.

This is not to say that you should use really long sentences all the time. Sometimes (like when you wish to suggest pace and excitement) short sentences are best.

Most pieces of writing are more interesting if you use a *variety* of sentence types.

A choice of conjunctions

To help you with the exercise on this page, here's a list of subordinating conjunctions you might wish to use:

If, after, where, before, because, until, though, as, when, unless, since, although, while

Try it yourself!

Alter the meaning

The conjunction you use can have a big effect on the meaning of the sentence. It can even tell you something about the characters involved.

Look at these two statements:

I went to the cinema. **There was a horror film showing.**

By your use of conjunctions, you can alter the whole sense. Choose a conjunction to fit with the instruction at the end of each line and write your completed sentences in your exercise book:

I went to the cinema ... there was a horror film showing. (You like horror films.)

I went to the cinema ... there was a horror film showing. (You dislike horror films.)

I went to the cinema ... there was a horror film showing. (You refuse to watch horror.)

I went to the cinema ... there was a horror film showing. (Horror is all you watch.)

Below are four sentences. All of them are complex sentences with two clauses joined by a conjunction (which may not be in the middle).

If the teacher asked me, I helped to collect in the books.

We had no hope of winning after Jane was dropped from the team.

We were in trouble until Ben joined the expedition.

I applied to Mayfield School because Mrs Schofield was the head.

Try a variety of conjunctions (check the list opposite) and write out all the sentences that you think make sense, explaining what sort of connection you have made; for example:

<u>Because</u> the teacher asked me, I helped to collect in the books. (gives a reason)

Alter the order of the clauses if you wish.

Compare your answers with those on **pages 45–48.** Your answers don't need to be identical, but you should now know something of the ways conjunctions join together compound and complex sentences.

Teacher's tips

Try to vary word order in sentences. Naturally, putting conjunctions first needs a following comma. Also, vary your use of simple, compound and complex sentences.

14

Full stops

Get started

A **full stop** does exactly what it says. It brings a sentence to a *full stop*. Writing without full stops would be very confusing.

Full stops can even alter the meaning of what you write. Read these sentences and see if you can tell the difference:

> **Eventually Seema arrived home half an hour before her father had to go to work.**

> **Eventually Seema arrived home. Half an hour before her father had to go to work.**

- What happened first?
- Did Seema arrive home before or after her father went to work?
- What is the importance of the full stop?

In the first sentence, Seema arrived home first; in the second, her father left first. If you need to check why, look at the **Still unsure?** note on the right.

Separating statements

A **full stop** goes between two separate statements. It marks the end of a sentence, and a capital letter marks the beginning of a new sentence.

A sentence is a group of words that makes complete sense on its own.

Still unsure?

- In the second example, the full stop completely separates the two halves: Seema arrived home and her father went to work *before* that happened.
- In the first example, the two are joined together, telling us that Seema arrived *before* her father left.

Practice

Take a look at these simple examples of the use of full stops:

> **The school bell rang. We all went back to our classes.**

> **I left my English homework till last. It's not my favourite subject.**

> **It snowed heavily on Monday. All the trains were cancelled.**

These are all very short sentences and there are no words to join the first and second halves together – so you need to *separate them with a full stop*.

This section looks at sentences which are **statements**. This means they tell the reader something. Not all sentences are statements and not all end in full stops. Later sections will explain this.

15

What is a sentence?

- A sentence must have a **verb**, a word of *doing* (like *caught*) or *being* (like *was*).
- It also has a **subject**, the person or thing doing (like *Katie*) or being (like *Jamie*).
- Two or more sentences can be joined together into one by words like *when*, *where*, *and*, *but*, *if*, *because* and so on. They become parts of the same sentence.
- So, *when he arrived at the airport* is not a separate sentence, but part of the sentence Jamie was amazed **when** he arrived at the airport.

Try it yourself!

Where's the full stop?

Find the right place for the full stop in the following examples and then write out the pairs of sentences in your exercise book:

> **I caught the bus from school to the station I had to walk the last mile home.**
>
> **The concert was sold out well in advance we had no chance of getting tickets.**
>
> **Mrs Jackson could not decide between Malta and Cyprus the travel agent recommended Malta.**
>
> **Jamie was amazed when he arrived at the airport his best friend was on the same flight.**
>
> **Katie left her books at school she said she couldn't do her homework.**

The answers are on **pages 45–48**. Did you get them all right?

If you are not sure, read **What is a sentence?** very carefully.

Where's the full stop?

Here are some simple sentences. At the end of each is a full stop followed by the subject of another sentence. Create a short sentence to finish off each example and write it in your exercise book.

> **The flight was delayed again. My father …**
>
> **I have never seen such a boring match. The goalkeepers …**
>
> **My favourite programme is 'EastEnders'. The last episode …**
>
> **We went on holiday to Tenerife. The weather …**

There are no answers given on **pages 45–48** as there are so many possible correct ones. Are you confident that yours are correct?

Remember:

- Your sentence must start with a capital letter.
- Your sentence should have a verb, e.g. **My father blamed the airline.** or **The weather was wonderful.**
- Your sentence must end with a full stop.

Teacher's tips

When writing longer pieces, think out sentences before you write them. The longer the sentence, the more likely you will need punctuation to break it up for the reader. Do not rely solely on proof-reading when you have finished the writing. Do it as you go!

More about full stops

Get started

A full stop goes between two separate statements. The problem is that some sentences are much longer than the ones examined so far. When several statements are joined together, you have to decide when the sentence comes to a *full stop*.

Look at this example:

> **We overtook an old Morris Minor on the M1. It looked in good condition.**

These are two short, separate statements with a full stop between them. What if some linked statements are added to both of them?

> **When we were driving down to London, we overtook an old Morris Minor on the M1 just before we came to the M25. So far as I could see, it looked in good condition, though it was only crawling along.**

All the added bits have been joined on with connecting words like *when* and *though*, and with added **commas** to help the reader take pauses. But nothing has been done to join up the two original sentences, so there is still a full stop between them.

Practice

A sentence should stand and make sense on its own:

> **The Mayor organised the charity appeal.**

There are other ways to write the same information that do not make sense on their own:

- *When the Mayor organised the charity appeal* – *when* is a link to something else which is not there.
- *Organising the charity appeal* – this does not say who is doing it.

So these last two are not sentences and do not need full stops. See if the following examples make this clear:

> **The Mayor organised the charity appeal. The council supported him.**
> **When the Mayor organised the charity appeal, the council supported him.**
> **Organising the charity appeal, the Mayor relied on the council for support.**

Another use for full stops?

Sometimes rules in English change and this is happening with full stops at the moment. A few years ago, the United States of America would have been shortened to U.S.A.; now it is written as USA, without full stops after the initials. This style is now quite correct, but the old form can still be used.

The old rule says that a full stop comes after an initial or a shortened version of a word (an **abbreviation**). Here are a few examples:

Mr. E. Davis	*Mr.* short for *Mister*; *E.* an initial
Ltd.	short for *Limited*
M.P.	initials for *Member of Parliament*
i.e.	short for two Latin words meaning 'that is' (not 'for example')
G.W.R.	initials of *Great Western Railway*

But beware …

In the cases above, you can use full stops if you wish or leave them out – but be consistent.

However, there is one common error to avoid.

The spelling *etc.* is short for *et cetera* (meaning 'and the rest'), not a set of initials, so *e.t.c.* is wrong and always has been – unless it stood for *Epsom Theatre Company*.

Placing full stops

You might have made sense of the activity **Fit them together** by using a slightly different arrangement of statements. If so, well done! Your version is probably right, too.

There are five statements that make sense on their own:

Mrs Harrison rushed into the room. She was obviously in a hurry. There was no room on the shelf. I could see my book on top of the pile. So I took them off her.

All the other statements support these – they do not make sense on their own. *When the bell rang* and *before she dropped them all* need to be joined to something else.

The last two statements form one sentence, joined together by *so*. Words like *so*, *and*, *or* and *but* join together equal statements.

Try it yourself!

Fit them together

Find the activity on **page 25**.

Twelve groups of words are provided, some complete statements, some not. Cut them all out and group them together in ways that make sense. You should end up with four sentences that follow on from each other. When you have done this, copy the sentences out in your exercise book and make absolutely certain that your full stops are in the right place!

Now check the answers on **pages 45–48**.

All correct?

If not, study the note **Placing full stops** on the left.

Where do you put the full stop?

The following examples contain two or more sentences each. There is already a full stop at the end of each one. Copy them into your exercise book and, as you do so, you must decide where else to place full stops to divide each example into two or more sentences. Try to put in other punctuation, like commas.

> **If you turn left into the town centre you pass the cinema the car park is just opposite.**
>
> **Sanjay moved to a new school in September he is enjoying it but he says there is too much homework.**
>
> **Where the river bends there is an old boathouse I will meet you there after you have visited your aunt we can go fishing.**

Now check the answers on **pages 45–48**.

All correct?

If not, try to think which statements make sense on their own. They need to be separated by full stops or joined together by a word like *and*, *but* or *so*. Remember what the note **Placing full stops** on the left says about this.

The last example might read, in its simplest form:

> **There is an old boathouse. I will meet you there. We can go fishing.**

Teacher's tips

Full stops, commas, connectives, types of sentence: these are choices that good writers need to juggle and be aware of at all times. Think about your reader and the purpose of your writing to help you make the right choices.

Question marks and exclamation marks

Get started

Are all sentences statements?

Of course not. Sentences can be **questions**, **commands** or **exclamations**.

These often need a different punctuation mark at the end.

Practice

What is a question?

This might seem obvious, but which of the following should end with a **question mark**?

> I wonder if the train is running late
> Would you mind moving your bags

The first one is asking for an answer as much as the second (perhaps more), but the rule is:

If a sentence is *in the form of a question*, it must end in a question mark.

So the correct punctuation is:

> I wonder if the train is running late.
> Would you mind moving your bags?

What are commands and exclamations?

- A command is an order.
- An exclamation is something that is expressed loudly or vigorously because of surprise or anger, perhaps. It is often a set phrase like *Good Heavens!*

Any exclamation is followed by an **exclamation mark**. A command might be followed by a full stop or an exclamation mark.

What is the difference between these two sentences?

> Close the door, please.
> Close that door!

Both are commands. The second is more emphatic and less polite – the exclamation mark expresses that.

Remember the rules:

- Use a question mark at the end of a sentence in question form.
- Use an exclamation mark after an exclamation or at the end of a very emphatic command.

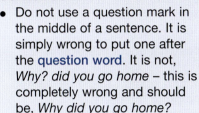

Always at the end of a sentence?

- Do not use a question mark in the middle of a sentence. It is simply wrong to put one after the **question word**. It is not, *Why? did you go home* – this is completely wrong and should be, *Why did you go home?*
- Sometimes exclamations are not full sentences. In this case, put the exclamation mark after the exclamation and follow with a capital letter:

  Oh, no! She's left her mobile on the bus.

- Sometimes, in conversation, a question might not be a complete sentence. *Why?* might be a perfectly correct reply to *I think I'll go home.*

Wait and see

In speech, where does the question mark or exclamation mark go in relation to the speech marks? This can be difficult. See the section **Punctuating speech** on **page 37**.

Question marks or not?

Remember that a question mark ends a sentence that is in the form of a question.

So what about this example?

Laura asked Craig if he wanted to go to the party.

Is the sentence telling the reader something or asking them something?

It tells the reader that Laura asked Craig; the sentence is a statement, ending in a full stop.

And please, avoid sentences like, **Laura asked Craig did he want to go to the party?** This is just *wrong*.

How about this?

In the third round, Wrexham were drawn at home to Manchester United. Everybody expected an away win and United attacked throughout the first half. However, in the second half the home team actually took the lead!

Try it yourself!

Which punctuation mark?

Before you try this exercise, read the text under **What is a question?** on the previous page.

Copy the following sentences into your exercise book, putting a full stop or a question mark at the end of each one:

> **Our flight is due to leave at 10 o'clock**
> **When is our flight due to leave**
> **Would you mind passing me the chocolates**
> **I wonder if you would pass me the chocolates**
> **I asked you if you would pass me the chocolates**
> **When does next term begin**
> **I wonder who will take us for English next term**

Turn to **pages 45–48** to check your answers.

All correct?

If you made any mistakes, look at them again and remember: if the sentence is in the form of a question, end it with a **question mark**.

What's the difference?

Ordinary sentences can end in exclamation marks if the person writing or speaking wants to be emphatic. For instance, a speaker might be annoyed; a writer might want to suggest surprise. Here are three ordinary sentences. In each case, try to think of a situation where an exclamation mark would be suitable. Write a short paragraph in your exercise book which includes the sentence ending in an exclamation mark.

> **In the second half, the home team actually took the lead.**
> **I have no intention of giving him a good report.**
> **Give out the exercise books.**

For one possible example, look at the note **How about this?** on the left.

Teacher's tips

Notice how exclamation marks often follow verbs of command (imperative verbs) e.g. *Stop! Wait for me!* A writer can overuse them though. Avoid making things seem surprising or shocking by peppering your writing with exclamation marks. Use them carefully and purposefully.

Colons and semicolons

Get started

Do you know the difference between **colons** and **semicolons**?

They look very similar, but have different jobs in a sentence, so you need to make sure that you remember the difference:

- A colon looks like two full stops on top of each other (:).
- A semicolon looks like a full stop above a comma (;).

Practice

The first thing to remember about semicolons is *not to worry*. Punctuation can be perfectly accurate without a semicolon in sight.

So why read on?

Using semicolons can make your work more stylish and give you a useful punctuation mark somewhere between a full stop and a comma:

Full stop	**Semicolon**	**Comma**
The sense comes to a full stop. Use a capital letter and start again.	The sense comes to a stop. The phrases before and after the semicolon are closely linked in meaning, not by connecting words.	There is a brief pause. The sense before and after the comma is joined by connecting words.

Examine the following example.

Take these two sentences:

> **Mrs Jackson enjoyed teaching GCSE.**
> **Mrs Robins preferred Key Stage 3.**

There are three ways you can present them:

- Leave them as they are – perfectly correct, but, if you use too many short sentences in your writing, it becomes boring.
- Use a comma – but you will need to add a connecting word, such as *while* at the beginning or *but* in the middle.
- Use a semicolon – the two sentences are so close in meaning they could be two halves of the same sentence: **Mrs Jackson enjoyed teaching GCSE; Mrs Robins preferred Key Stage 3.**

If you have any doubt, play safe and avoid semicolons until you are confident.

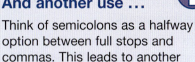

And another use …

Think of semicolons as a halfway option between full stops and commas. This leads to another possible use – in a list.

The section on **Commas** on page 29 explains that commas are used between the items in a list. But what if the items in the list are long and contain commas themselves?

Read the following example showing another possible use of semicolons:

When I went on holiday, I made sure I took warm clothes because it gets cold in Scotland in the autumn; my compass, maps and guide books in case I had the chance to go hiking; my mp3 player and batteries; my English books, though I didn't really expect to do any schoolwork, and, of course, my mobile phone.

Full stops or semicolons?

It is clear why three of the sentences in Using the semicolon need a comma in the middle. In each case, a connecting word has joined the two statements: *but* and *so* in the middle, *when* at the beginning.

There is more choice in the other four cases. In each case, a full stop would not be wrong, but these are the reasons for the choice made here:

- The first and second coaches are linked together in meaning. So are the two different parts of the view. So a semicolon seems like a good idea.
- There is less direct connection in the other two examples (the evening's activities and rooms are very different things), so full stops seem more suitable.

More on semicolons

The next section on page 27 is on colons, but the exercises include an activity on colons and semicolons. If you still feel you need more practice on how to use semicolons, wait and see if the activity helps.

Try it yourself!

Using the semicolon

There is a break in the middle of each of the following examples. Decide whether to use a full stop, a comma or a semicolon.

> **We all thought the school expedition would be fun but the weather spoiled everything.**

> **The first coach set off at 9 o'clock the second one waited for the latecomers.**

> **When we arrived at the hostel the thunder and lightning started.**

> **The evening's activities were cancelled we found the rooms were very comfortable.**

> **The building was on top of a hill so we had a good view of the surrounding countryside.**

> **There was a river valley below us I could just see woodland on the far side.**

> **We decided to make the best of it this would be home for the next three days.**

Compare your answers with those on **pages 45–48**.

All correct?

If not, read the explanations in **Full stops or semicolons?** on the left.

Create your own

Below are two statements. Copy each one into your exercise book. Then try to think of three other statements to write after each one: the first preceded by a comma, the second by a semicolon and the third by a full stop. The first one is done for you.

> **The new sports hall should be finished by September**, but the official opening is not until November.

> **I am going to see my favourite group next month**

Remember:

- You need a joining or connecting word with a comma.
- Following a semicolon, the next statement should be strongly connected in meaning with the one before. In the first example above, it might be about some other building work at the school.

Teacher's tips

As your writing improves, and your sentences get longer and more complex, avoid overusing the comma and semicolon. Good writers make good choices.

22

Activities

Put them together (page 6)

Below are nouns, pronouns, noun phrases and verbs all jumbled together. Cut them out and put them in separate piles. The nouns, pronouns and noun phrases can all be subjects, direct objects or indirect objects. By moving the words and phrases around, make as many sentences as you can. Write out in your exercise book:

- sentences where you can reverse subject and object, for example:
  The lion frightened the hunter. The hunter frightened the lion.
- sentences with both direct and indirect objects.

the lion	what to do	I	the bus
gave	him	caught	a chance
offered	frightened	knew	the hunter
a medal	the late goal	won	praised
celebrated	the mayor	wondered	a fight
the architect	my brother	awarded	followed
the quarrel	whether to go	worried	the new tram
outperformed	you	paid	his fee

23

Activities

Mixing the sentences (page 10)

Below you will find a mixture of parts of sentences. Some are verbs, so you will know what their part in a sentence will be. Some are nouns or noun phrases, so they could be subjects or objects or complements. Adjectives will need a noun to relate to and adverbs will probably be used with a verb, adjective or adverb.

You will probably find it easiest to start with all the words and phrases in piles according to parts of speech. Then create, and write out in your exercise book, four sentences:

1 with a verb of being and complement
2 with a verb of doing, direct and indirect objects
3 as 1, but with at least one adverb or adverb phrase
4 as 2, but with at least one adverb or adverb phrase.

Then assemble as many words and phrases as you can to create the longest sentence that makes sense.

every May	in the park	carefully	brought
was smiling	Mr Shah	happy	his lorry
across the river	in a temper	they	were
became	gently	seems	too late
Tony	quietly	offered	the school
in the garden	gave	the children	after work
advice	in the rain	at five o'clock	I
shouted	a party	a warning	generously

24

Activities

Fit them together (page 18)

Here are twelve groups of words. Cut them all out and group them together in ways that make sense. You should end up with four sentences that follow on from each other. Then copy them out in your exercise book.

- when the bell rang
- I could see my book on top of the pile
- because she never even noticed
- Mrs Harrison rushed into the room
- from where I was sitting
- there was no room on the shelf
- she was obviously in a hurry
- before she dropped them all
- carrying a pile of exercise books
- that half the class was missing
- where she always puts our books
- so I took them off her

Activities

The commas game (page 30)

Many of the following words and phrases have a comma, either at the beginning or at the end. Cut out the words and phrases and use the commas to help you arrange them into a piece of writing that makes sense. You need to supply your own full stops, but the capital letters at the start of sentences have been included to help you.

Not surprisingly,

, over 50 people applying for 20 places

, but the team was on a pre-season tour of Portugal

In July last year,

Mike Stratton,

hoped some United players would help out

numbers on the other two

All those who took part received four hours a day coaching,

, practical science and various sports

While the road safety course was also full up,

the course on football was very popular

a snack lunch,

, first aid and practical science

, presented on the final afternoon

while the school was closed for ordinary lessons

, first aid

, were disappointing

a football video and a certificate

The organiser of the course,

, the council decided to run courses in road safety

26

More about colons

Get started

Unlike a **semicolon**, a **colon** has a very clear job in the middle of a sentence – or rather, it has three similar jobs:

- A colon can introduce a list in the second part of the sentence.
- A colon can come before a more detailed expansion of the first half.
- A colon can come before an explanation of the first half.

Practice

These examples will make it clearer:

> We have five different subjects on Monday: Science, English, French, Drama and Art.

> It was a real mess in the hall: some windows were broken, the curtains were torn and there was glass all over the place.

> It was a real mess in the hall: at the height of the storm, a tree had blown down outside and smashed the windows next to the stage.

- The first example is straightforward: the colon introduces *a list*.
- The second gives *more details* of the mess in the hall (broken windows, torn curtains, glass).
- The third gives *an explanation* of how the mess was caused (a tree had blown down outside, etc.).

Still not sure?

Think of it this way: if the first half of the sentence leaves you thinking, 'I need to know more', or 'What next?', it is probably a job for the colon, introducing more facts or giving an explanation.

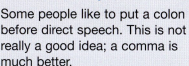

Colons and speech

Some people like to put a colon before direct speech. This is not really a good idea; a comma is much better.

However, colons can be used for quotations.

Have you ever written about a Shakespeare play and needed to quote a speech? Or written about a poem and quoted some lines? That is when you can use a colon:

The witches in *Macbeth* say a strange rhyme when they are casting their spells:

> 'Double double, toil and trouble;
>
> Fire burn and cauldron bubble.'

Teacher's tips

Subject text books (like science or geography) often use colons when providing information, examples and explanations. Notice these. Work out how they are being used. Use them not just in English but in other subjects. Colons before lists are the ones most remembered. Focus on colons before explanations or clarifications.

27

Some ideas for 'What follows a colon?'

- A list of Jamie's offences (truancy, cheek, chewing in class) is easy enough.
- For added detail, you could put: last week he even got sent off in a school football match.
- For explanation, you could have something like: his mother thought he just liked to be the centre of attention.

For the second example, you could have:
- a list of places
- last year we went to Portugal as well as Disneyworld.
- my father thinks we'd all get bored if we went to the same place again.

There's no dash

Some people like to follow a colon with a dash when introducing a list (:-).

This is a bit old-fashioned so just use the colon on its own.

Try it yourself!

Matching up the statements

List A consists of eight statements, each the first half of a sentence. List B consists of eight possible clauses or phrases to finish the sentence. For each item in List A, complete the sentence in different ways. Decide whether a colon or semi colon is better for each sentence.

List A

> I found an old coin in the garden
> The school bus was late again
> I always worried about my music lesson
> We buy most things at the supermarket
> The journey took three hours
> I decided to leave the orchestra
> We organised a collection for charity
> I tried to find a really good hiding place

List B

> I never practised enough
> it was over 100 years old
> food, clothes, household goods and even books
> there were miles of road works
> my friends looked for one, too
> it's always such good value
> we all missed school assembly
> we usually go down in the car

You may think that 'there were miles of road works' can follow 'The journey took three hours.' The second part is an explanation of the first – and that means a colon, so you write down, 'The journey took three hours: there were miles of road works.'

Find as many examples as you can; use List B as often as you want.

Some statements can be paired with more than one example. Remember to distinguish between:

Colon   statement + list, or statement + detail, or statement + explanation

Semicolon two connected statements

So: **The school bus was late again: there were miles of road works.** (explanation)

Or: **The school bus was late again; we all missed school assembly.** (linked statements)

What follows a colon?

Create your own endings to these sentences. You should write three for each sentence in your exercise book: one list, one enlargement (more detail), one explanation:

> Jamie found many ways of getting into trouble:
> We always like to go to different places on holiday:

Some ideas are given in the note at the top left. Complete your own versions before you look.

Commas

Get started

The **comma** is unusual among punctuation marks because *most people use it far too often*. The first rules to learn about the comma might be:

- Do not use it between two separate statements – that is the job of a full stop or perhaps a semicolon.
- Do not use it to break up a simple statement, question or command.
- Remember that sometimes the use of a comma is a matter of choice.

So what is a comma for?

The simplest explanation is:

A comma indicates a *pause* in writing, not a stop.

Compare it to pausing in speech, for breath, emphasis or to make sense of what is being said.

Practice

A comma has many jobs, all indicating a small difference between the words and phrases on each side of it:

- *Lists* – between the words or phrases in a list
- *Listeners* – after or before the name of the person being spoken to
- *Speech* – between the speaker and the words spoken
- *Clauses and phrases* – to separate different parts of a sentence.

In the next section, **More about commas**, there is a much fuller account of each of these jobs.

For now, learn the first rule of commas:

Commas should reduce confusion. A comma tells the reader to make a little gap between the words or phrases before and after the comma.

The disappearing comma

Until recently, there would have been some definite jobs for commas in letter writing:
- After the house number and each line of the address
- After *Dear Sir, Dear Aunt Julia, Yours sincerely* or *Yours faithfully*
- Between month and year in the date: *29th February, 1996*

If you look at letters now, you will not usually find commas in these places. It is not wrong to use a comma like this, but it is rather out-of-date.

Don't break up the sense

When the tickets go on sale, there will be crowds of fans at the box office.

In this sentence, the comma is used to separate two statements which have been joined by a connecting word (*when*).

But look at another sentence:

I don't know when the tickets go on sale.

There is no comma here because *when the tickets go on sale* is part of the main sense of the sentence; it forms the direct object.

So the rule is: do not break up the sense with a comma.

Helpful hints

The commas game opposite is quite a complicated exercise. Can you work out the right order?

Remember one or two rules that might help:

- Commas are used to separate items in a list – except for the last one following *and*. So, with a phrase like 'a football video and a certificate', this might be the end of a list. If so, the phrase before it must end in a comma.
- Connecting words like *but* follow a mid-sentence comma, so, 'but the team was on a pre-season tour of Portugal' is likely to be the second half of a sentence. Find the first half: without a comma, of course, as that is already there.
- A clause like 'while the school was closed for ordinary lessons' needs a comma before and after (it is not the start of a sentence), so look for suitable phrases beginning and ending with commas.

Right or wrong?

One possible variation from the version given on **pages 45–48**:

You may have placed the last sentence earlier in the piece. This could also make sense, though at the end is probably the best place for it.

Try it yourself!

The commas game

Turn to the activity on **page 26**.

You will find a list of phrases that, when joined together, make a continuous piece of writing.

Cut out all the words and phrases and then move them around until you have a piece of writing that makes sense. The placing of the commas should help you.

When you are happy with your version, write it out in your exercise book.

Beware: Other punctuation marks are not included; remember to add your own full stops, etc.

Check your version with the one on **pages 45–48**.

All correct?

If not, compare the two versions and try to work out where you went wrong or whether your version makes equally good sense.

Still unsure?

Read the next section for more help.

Teacher's tips

Do not overuse commas. Think about the sense of the sentence. Would you pause when reading it aloud? Remember - additional information can be surrounded by commas e.g. *Sarah, the student, wrote carefully.* Also, opening connectives often have one, just like *'also'* in this sentence!

More about commas

Get started

Use a comma between the various items in a list, except for the last one with the word *and*: **I entered for the 100 metres, the 200 metres, the high jump and the relay.**

Some points to bear in mind:

- If you have very long items in the list, you might prefer to use a semicolon.
- In some cases (if, perhaps, the word *and* occurs more than once), you *might* choose to put a comma before the last item: **Bring with you the map, your compass, your coat and gloves, and your packed lunch.**
- Careful use of commas in lists matters. How many boys are here: two, three, four or five? **Mike Leslie Grant Lee and Barry** Only commas can make clear whether there is someone called *Mike Leslie* or *Leslie Grant* or *Grant Lee* or none of these.

Practice

A comma introduces speech. After *He said* or *She whispered*, put a comma before the words spoken. The same thing applies if the phrase comes at the end of the speech and, usually, if it comes in the middle:

'The trouble with you,' Sally said, 'is that you never pay attention.'

The sections on speech punctuation (**pages 37–40**) give full details.

Commas also indicate separate phrases or clauses. Here are two separate statements:

The flight was due to take off. We were still at the check-in desk.

When we join separate statements together with a connecting word, we use a comma:

When the flight was due to take off, we were still at the check-in desk.

The flight was due to take off, but we were still at the check-in desk.

You should mark off a separate phrase with commas at the beginning and the end:

The steeply sloping path, going down to the valley floor, was filled with boulders.

or

The steeply sloping path, filled with boulders, went down to the valley floor.

Commas for listeners

If you identify the person or people you are speaking to, separate the name or title from the rest of the sentence with a comma or commas:

Members of the Church Council, it gives me great pleasure to be here.

Now you're here, Joanna, let's listen to your CD.

So what is the difference between the following two sentences?

All contestants in the sprint relay stand over there.

And

All contestants in the sprint relay, stand over there.

The first is a statement, telling what the contestants do.

The second is a command, telling the contestants to take their positions.

31

Joined with a comma?

As already mentioned, some words join together two equal sentences: *and*, *but*, *so* and *or* are the main ones.

Is a comma needed where the sentences join?

That depends on the connecting word:

but/so   comma
or   no comma
and   usually no comma

I went to the school office, but I couldn't find the register.

I went to the school office and collected the register.

A last word on commas

- Always use common sense.
- Do not over-use commas.
- Always use a comma if the meaning is not clear without one.

Try it yourself!

Where are the commas?

In the piece of writing below, all the punctuation marks are included, except for commas. Copy the piece into your exercise book, writing in commas where they are needed – and, just as important, making sure that you do not include any unnecessary commas.

> When you start a piece of homework it is important to make sure that you have everything you need: books pens paper and if necessary a calculator. You should decide when is the best time to start work. If you have younger brothers and sisters it is a good idea to choose a time when they are out playing visiting friends or doing their own work. You do not want to be interrupted by your sister saying 'Come on Kirsty have a look at this on television.' Your concentration on your work even if you are doing something exciting like English can suffer but you must try not to be distracted.
>
> Finally you have everything you need and the house is really quiet. You open your textbook find the right page check the question you have to answer and make a start. For the next hour except for when you get a drink from the kitchen you are hard at work.

Check the correct version on **pages 45–48**.

All correct?

No? Then try a different way of thinking about commas.

Read the last sentence of the first paragraph again. It is confusing without punctuation.

There are three statements all linked together:

> your concentration on your work can suffer
>
> even if you are doing something exciting like English
>
> but you must try not to be distracted

By using commas you can make them linked-but-separate.

Think of commas as road signs for meaning, showing the reader where to go.

Teacher's tips

Read longer, complex sentences back to yourself. Be alert to a change of topic or meaning, a need to pause. But also do not overuse commas. It can be tricky, so always be thinking about it when you are writing.

Dashes, hyphens and brackets

Get started

Previous pages have dealt with the main punctuation marks in a sentence:

- *Terminal points* (that is, marks that go at the end of a sentence) which are mostly *full stops*, but include special marks to end *questions* and *exclamations*.
- *Colons* to introduce lists, details and explanations; *semicolons* to act as a gentler full stop.
- *Commas* for all the small pauses, never to separate unconnected statements.

If you are in any doubt about any of these, go back and remind yourself of the relevant section before moving on.

Practice

Like commas, colons and semicolons, a **dash** indicates a break in a sentence. The sort of break a dash marks is generally an informal one, something that breaks up the smooth flow of a sentence. There are three main uses for a dash:

- If a sentence is interrupted, mostly in speech, use a dash: **The receptionist said, 'I don't think Mr Singh will see – ' 'He will when he knows what it's about,' I interrupted.** (If the sentence just peters out, use …)
- If you want to put in an informal break, for humour or excitement, use a dash: **Steve saw his big chance, raced onto the loose ball, beat the fullback, cut into the area, set up the shooting chance – and missed the ball completely!**
- The main use for dashes is to mark **parentheses** (the plural of *parenthesis*). When you drop in a part of a sentence without really connecting it to the rest, you can punctuate it with dashes: **It's difficult enough having your friend to stay in the holidays – it's only a small house after all and we have your grandma to think of – without having extra visitors each day.** Note: you can use brackets instead of dashes for this. It is a matter of choice.

What does it look like?

A **dash** and a **hyphen** can look the same; ideally a dash should be longer. If you are using a computer, try to find the correct key combination that will give you a dash and, if you are writing by hand, try to make a difference. The uses of dashes and hyphens are, in fact, totally different:

- A dash has various tasks within the sentence, mainly to indicate parenthesis. Also, if you are making informal notes, you might use a dash to indicate breaks.
- A hyphen links together two or more words to form what is called a **compound**: *red-haired, bad-tempered, left-handed*.

More commas

Much of this section deals with the use of parenthesis. This is when an extra, unconnected phrase is inserted in a sentence. Brackets or dashes are often used for this. However, if the parenthesis is short, it can be yet another job for the comma:

The first chapter was so long and difficult, never mind the whole book, that I nearly gave up.

This is a matter of choice. Brackets or dashes would not be wrong.

Work in pairs

Once you open a bracket, remember to close it after the parenthesis, even if it is at the end of a sentence. With a parenthesis, dashes also work in pairs, but never finish a sentence with a dash.

Some suggestions

- The football match could be *close-fought*, *high-scoring*, *heart-stopping*, *nerve-tingling* …
- The parenthesis could come after *The best holiday I have ever had*. For a short one, with commas, you could try: *not that I've had many*. An extended one might be something like: (*and I'm including that time we visited our cousins in America and toured California*).
- You need Tom interrupting with remarks like *But I'm rubbish at drama*, and then saying such things as *I don't know, Miss, maybe*…
- Try this: **We reached the landing which was musty and full of cobwebs. As we looked around, the air seemed to get colder, we heard a strange noise – and the bedroom door swung open.**

Try it yourself!

Make your own examples

In this exercise, you need to create your own examples in your exercise book to show the use of hyphens, dashes and brackets. There are, of course, no correct answers to these. Some suggestions are given in the note on the left.

- Use hyphens to link two or three compound adjectives to describe a football match that finished 3–3 with both teams competing fiercely.
- Read the sentence: **The best holiday I have ever had was when we went to Greece for a fortnight**. Now write it out, adding a short parenthesis using commas.
  Now add a longer parenthesis with brackets or dashes.
- Write a brief conversation in play form where Mrs Desai is trying to persuade Tom to be in the school play. Use at least one interruption, indicated by a dash, and at least one sentence which just peters out, indicated by a series of three dots.
- Write two sentences from an exciting story about exploring a mysterious old house. Use a dash to build tension and indicate a scary moment.

How did your examples compare with the ideas given?

Remember that they do not have to be the same.

Still unsure?

You will probably not use dashes and brackets very much in your writing (too many parentheses are not a good idea anyway), but try following this advice:

- If you want to insert a bit extra in a sentence, just a little bit, use commas.
- If you want to insert something in a sentence – and it might cause confusion, because it is so long and there are already so many commas – use dashes or brackets.

Teacher's tips

Most pauses and extra information in your sentences will need commas. Now and again you might use a dash or a bracket. Only use these last two when you are sure (that is, very sure – very certain).

34

Apostrophes

Get started

In the following examples a letter has been left out, sometimes more than one. Where the letter should be, there is an **apostrophe**:

> The driver didn't see me at the bus stop.
> Most children enjoy Hallowe'en.
> We'll be late for school.

The letter left out in the first sentence is *o*, in the third there are two letters: *wi*. The term 'Hallowe'en' comes from the Eve of All Saints' (All Hallows') Day, Hallow even(ing).

Apostrophes often appear where the word *not* should be. We tend to say *not* quickly, so *do not* becomes *don't*. The apostrophe is used in place of the letter *o*.

Note: There are one or two unusual words to learn: *won't* (for *will not*) and *shan't* (for *shall not*).

Practice

An apostrophe followed by an *s* shows possession or belonging.
Look at the difference between *teachers* and *teacher's*.
The first means 'more than one' (*plural*), the second means 'belonging to one':

> The teachers held a meeting at lunchtime.
> My teacher's car broke down on the way to school.

What if you want to say, 'belonging to more than one'? First of all, put the *s* for plural, then the apostrophe for belonging, but leave out the extra *s*:

> All the teachers' cars were parked next to the school.

What is an apostrophe?

Look carefully at the spelling of **apostrophe** and check you can write it correctly. It is pronounced 'a-*pos*-tro-phy' and it looks like a comma in the air: my mother's car or I can't find my watch.

An apostrophe has two main uses:
- to show where a letter has been left out
- to show belonging or possession (with the letter *s*).

Whose is it?

To show possession or belonging, start with the 'owner'. This may be one person/thing (*car*) or more than one (*cars*). Add an apostrophe to show possession, then add an *s*.

The car's tyres were flat.

If there are two cars, the apostrophe still comes after the end of the word. But should there be a second *s*? The answer is to use common sense. It would sound silly to say, The cars's tyres were flat, so leave out the second *s*:

Both the cars' tyres were flat.

35

Problems with the final *s*

Some words end in *s* anyway. When you want to show that a *bus* or your *class* or *James* owns something, do you put an extra *s* after the apostrophe? To some extent, this is up to you:

- What matters here is how you say it.
- If you make an extra *s* sound, write an extra *s*.
- If you say 'That is *Jameses* book', you can write *James's*.

Problems with plurals

Most plurals end in *s*, but there are many exceptions: *children*, *women*, *sheep*, *feet* and so on. In these cases, use the apostrophe followed by *s* in the ordinary way: *children's clothing* – not *childrens' clothing*

Try it yourself!

Apostrophes for letters

Copy these sentences into your exercise book, but replace the words in italics with a shortened version using an apostrophe:

It has been very cold today.

If *I am* lucky, *I will* get to the match.

She *did not* call after all.

Claire *will not* change her mind.

He is willing to play if Aneeta *cannot*.

Check your answers on **pages 45–48. All correct?**
Remember:

Put the apostrophe where the letters are left out, not between the words.

So:

I didn't make a mistake. right

I did'nt make a mistake. wrong

Apostrophes mean belonging

How many of these phrases need an apostrophe before the *s*?
Write the correct versions in your exercise book:

Sarahs mobile phone | five miles to go

cauliflowers for sale | the schools reputation

fish and chips | passengers this way

the groups leader | my friends name

All correct? Then try these more difficult examples. Most involve plurals and possession:

womens rights | Charles Dickens novels

both boats oars | two pounds worth

a girls school | childrens books

Check your answers to all of the above on **pages 45–48**.

If any of your answers were wrong, get more practice by checking the notes on the left.

Teacher's tips

Shortened words like *it's* or *didn't* may only be necessary in writing speech. Elsewhere, use the full form of *it is* and *did not*. The tricky one is the apostrophe for plural possession. Remember that you only need the apostrophe if something belongs to somebody e.g. *Simon's books*.

36

Punctuating speech

Get started

There is special punctuation for **direct speech**, but not for **indirect** (or **reported**) **speech**. If you are unsure about the difference, read the note on the right, **Indirect or reported speech**.

Direct speech uses the exact words spoken, and there is a way of marking these words separate from the main piece of writing – otherwise the reader might think *I* was the writer, not the speaker.

Practice

Speech marks, quotation marks or inverted commas?

Which term does your teacher use? It does not really matter as they all refer to the same thing.

Do you prefer to use single marks (' ') or double (" ")? Both are correct; in this book we have used single speech marks. Here are some rules for using speech marks:

- Put the speech marks around the actual words spoken: **Lucy said, 'I don't want to go to the party.'**
- If you put *he said* or *she shouted* in the middle of the speech, close the speech marks and open them again: **'If they call for me,' Lucy said, 'say I'm not very well.'** Note where an extra comma has been added: more about that in **More about speech punctuation** in the next section.
- If you want to quote somebody else in the middle of a speech, use whichever speech marks you have *not* used so far (double or single): **Lucy explained, 'Nikki said, "We're coming round at about seven."'**
- If you open speech marks, you must close them: look at the last example and see how two sets were closed.

There are two simple rules:

- Be consistent with either double or single speech marks.
- Only use speech marks around the exact words spoken. Do not put them around *she said* or *he muttered* unless somebody (like Lucy above) actually spoke those words.

Are you unsure about using commas, question marks, etc., around speech? The next section deals with this.

Indirect or reported speech

In a story or in a report on a meeting, you may wish to write what somebody said. There are two ways of doing this:

- by writing down the exact words used. This is called **direct speech**.
- by making it part of your own story or report. You do not use the actual words. Instead you report it:

    Jason said that he had decided to go home.

    This is called **indirect** (or **reported**) **speech** and does not need special punctuation. Do not use any form of speech marks with reported speech.

Speech within speech

The use of double or single speech marks is purely a matter of choice. But always remember: for a speech inside a speech, use the other. So the example opposite could also be:

Lucy explained, "Nikki said, 'We're coming round at about seven.'"

Remember this

You can avoid most mistakes by remembering three rules:
- Put speech marks around the actual words spoken.
- Do not put speech marks round the *he said* part.
- Once opened, speech marks must be closed.

Some suggestions for 'Match the speakers'

There are no *correct* answers, but here are some ideas:

'If you don't come in now,' my father shouted, 'your dinner will get cold.'

Jarmila whispered, 'We did this work last term.'

'We've plenty of time,' Chloe said to her friend, 'so let's go to the shops after school.'

'I'm afraid you can't come in here,' answered the doorman.

'It's all right you saying that,' Ben replied, 'but I'm the one who has to tell him.'

Try it yourself!

Match the speakers

Here are five spoken sentences and five statements of who is speaking or replying.

If you don't come in now, your dinner will get cold.

We did this work last term.

We've plenty of time, so let's go to the shops after school.

I'm afraid you can't come in here.

It's all right you saying that, but I'm the one who has to tell him.

Answered the doorman

My father shouted

Jarmila whispered

Ben replied

Chloe said to her friend

Arrange these in suitable pairs: speaker and speech. Sometimes you might prefer the speaker to come first, sometimes the speech, or you might wish to divide the speech in the middle. Insert speech marks where necessary.

Place the speech marks

Copy the following sentences into your exercise book and see if you can find the right places to insert speech marks. All the other punctuation is correct and in the right place.

Anthony moaned, Tomorrow I've got to stay in and tidy my bedroom.

It could be worse, replied his sister, you might have had to cut the grass.

They asked me, said Anthony, but I said, You can't be serious!.

His sister told him to be quiet and stop making such a fuss.

Check your answers on **pages 45–48**.

All correct?

The fourth sentence needed no speech marks. Can you remember why? If not, turn back to **page 37** and look at the note on **Indirect or reported speech**.

Did the sentence contain the actual words spoken?

Teacher's tips

Lots to think about here! New speaker, new line. Speech marks round the words spoken. Fit in the other punctuation. *He said, 'Do not forget the comma between the words spoken and the writer's words 'he said'.'*

More about speech punctuation

Get started

As well as knowing how to use quotation/speech marks correctly, it is important to understand other punctuation around speech.

Practice

The correct punctuation mark to use between the speaker and the speech is the **comma**:

> Sonya said, 'It's time we went home.'
> 'It's time we went home,' Sonya said.
> 'If that's the time,' Sonya said, 'it's time we went home.'

Note that the comma is used whether *Sonya said* comes at the beginning, the middle or the end.

But watch out for the exception …

If the speaker is mentioned in the middle of the speech and if the first half is a full sentence, then use a full stop before the speech starts again.

This sounds complicated, but just follow these examples:

> 'I've finished with these files,' said the manager. 'You can clear them away now.'
> 'I've looked everywhere,' said the manager, 'but I can't find those files.'

If you need more practice, look at the note on **Commas and full stops** on the right.

Which comes first, the question/exclamation mark or the speech marks?

This problem also affects full stops, but it is always more noticeable with question marks and exclamation marks. Some people find it difficult, but the rule is very simple:

If the question or exclamation is part of the speech, put the mark *inside the speech marks*.

So: Faisal asked me, 'Have you brought the right books?'
     The new teacher shouted, 'This is disgraceful behaviour!'
But: Did she really say, 'I'm going out with Tony'?

Long speeches

Remember the rule that any speech marks you open must be closed again?

However, there is an exception when you have a really long speech lasting several paragraphs:
- If you do nothing, the reader might forget it is a speech.
- If you close the speech marks, that means the speech is over.
- So, in this case, repeat the speech marks at the start of each paragraph, but do not close them until the speech is over.

Commas and full stops

There has to be a bridge between *she said* or *he shouted* and the actual words spoken. This bridge is a comma.

But look again at the first example opposite about the manager and the files.

The manager speaks two separate sentences: his speech comes to a full stop and then starts again, and in this instance a full stop and a capital letter are used.

More on questions and exclamations

If a speech ends with a question, there are two punctuation marks together: one to show the question, one to show the end of the speech. Which one comes first?

Think it out for yourself.

Imagine the speech is in a play. You might write:

Juliet   Romeo, Romeo, wherefore art thou Romeo?

The question mark is part of the speech, so it goes inside the speech marks:

Juliet asked Romeo, 'Wherefore art thou Romeo?'

Who spoke?

Sometimes, usually when there are only two people in conversation, you can leave out the references to speakers and just put the words spoken. In that case, just use quotation marks normally – and *remember to take a new line for each speaker.*

Try it yourself!

Split in the middle

Copy the following speeches into your exercise book, but add *I said* to each of them, always placing it in the middle of the speech. Take very great care with your punctuation, not just quotation marks, but placing any commas, full stops, question marks and exclamation marks in the right places:

> When you get back from holiday, come round and see me.
>
> If you're so keen on football, why don't you come to the match tomorrow?
>
> The train was held up at Dunbar. That's why I'm so late.
>
> He's managed to lose his watch again. He's so silly!
>
> I never expected to be back in time, but the road was really clear.

Look at the answers on **pages 45–48**.

All correct?

If not, where was your mistake?
- In the placing of question marks and exclamation marks? Look at the note on the left for more explanation.
- In the use of commas and full stops? Go back to the two notes on **page 27** and read them closely.

Who said that?

Read the following examples and decide who made the final comment about the gymnasium and the classroom block. Then check on **pages 45–48**.

> 'We must take great care that we don't overspend on the new library,' said the Chair of Governors. 'There are many other projects for which we need money and, though the library is important, it wouldn't be right to pour all our funds into it.
>
>   'The gymnasium needs refurbishing and the old classroom block is in a very poor state.'

> 'We must take great care that we don't overspend on the new library,' said the Chair of Governors. 'There are many other projects for which we need money and, though the library is important, it wouldn't be right to pour all our funds into it.'
>
>   'The gymnasium needs refurbishing and the old classroom block is in a very poor state.'

Teacher's tips

The words spoken must begin with a capital letter. That is the beginning of the speaker's sentence. With long conversations, check that you do not overuse *'he said'* and *'she said'*. Make it clear who is speaking from the words you have put in the characters' mouths.

40

Summarising punctuation

Get started

Correct punctuation is needed to make sense of written English.

In speech, the speaker can pause or emphasise a word or phrase to help bring out the meaning.

In writing, punctuation marks tell the reader how our words and phrases fit together:

- Punctuation can mark the end of a sentence, a simple statement – **full stop**.
- The sentence may be a question or exclamation – **question mark** or **exclamation mark**.
- If two or more sentences are joined together by connecting words, it is often necessary to mark where they meet – **comma**.
- If two statements are very close in meaning, even without a connecting word, it seems wrong to start a new sentence – **semicolon**.
- The second part of a sentence may be a list or statement that explains or gives more information about the first half – **colon**.

If a sentence has something separate inserted in it:

- A parenthesis (an extra part not really part of the main sentence) is added – **brackets** or **dashes**.
- The added part may take the form of speech. If the exact words spoken are used, separate them from the main sentence – **speech marks/ quotation marks/inverted commas**.

Other jobs for punctuation

This page explains the main uses of punctuation in separating and joining sentences, and indicating the main parts of sentences. Here are some other points to remember:

- A **comma** has all sorts of useful little jobs. It separates words that we might otherwise confuse. So commas are placed between items in a list, when you mention the name of the person you are speaking to, and so on.
- Punctuation can happen inside words. **Hyphens** join words together. **Apostrophes** indicate missing letters or (with *s*) show possession or belonging.
- Though **speech marks** are very important, remember to support them with the correct use of other punctuation around speech.

Practice

Above is a simple summary of the rules of sentence punctuation. However, it is no good just learning them as rules and doing exercises correctly. You need to be able to use punctuation correctly – without having to think about it – in all your writing.

So the final punctuation exercise is rather different from the others. It asks you to make the right decisions in a fairly long piece of writing, without any hint of which punctuation mark is being tested.

Supporting punctuation

Here are five ways to support accurate punctuation:

- Do not forget the capital letter at the start of a sentence.
- On the other hand, do not overuse capital letters. Apart from starting sentences, they should only be used for individual names: *Laura*, *Grimsby* and *Arsenal*, but not *girl*, *town* or *team*.
- Remember to use apostrophes in the middle of words only if letters are left out. *It's* means *it is* or *it has*. It is wrong to put an apostrophe in *its* meaning 'belonging to it' (**The dog wagged its tail**).
- Starting a new line can sometimes make meaning clearer: a new speaker in direct speech, for instance.
- Do not forget to use paragraphs wisely.

Try it yourself!

A final test

What is most important is that you should be able to use all punctuation naturally and correctly in your everyday writing. Below is a story with no punctuation marks. Can you write it out correctly punctuated? You will need to decide where sentences end and where speech takes place.

> When we arrived at the station we all felt rather confused the timetable said the London train left from Platform 2 but the departure board said Platform 5 what shall we do said Tony theres no need to worry yet Anne replied the trains not due to leave for ten minutes I decided to see if I could buy a magazine for the journey I wasnt sure if I had time but Anne said the bookstall was just round the corner while I went to get a magazine the others decided to try to find someone to help us the result was that when I came back with my copy of Heat they were nowhere to be seen what a predicament there I was standing in the station entrance with no idea where my friends were or what platform the train went from and now there were only five minutes left I raced towards Platform 5 in a state of panic then just as I caught sight of Anne and Tony an announcement came over the loudspeaker owing to track repairs the 10.45 to London Euston is running late said the announcer and will now depart from Platform 7 at approximately 11.05

Compare your version to the one given on **pages 45–48**. How did you do?

Sometimes there is more than one correct answer. For example, the only essential exclamation mark is at the end of **What a predicament!**, but there are other possibilities and your version might be slightly different from the one given.

If there is anything you are unsure about, look it up in the section dealing with the relevant punctuation mark used.

Teacher's tips

When we speak, we use more than words to be understood: pauses, facial and hand gestures, emphasis, changes of tone as the voice goes up and down. Punctuation can be seen as a writer's way of doing these things. Keep all the punctuation marks in mind as you write. And do not overdo it.

Paragraphing

Get started

Punctuation is there to make meaning clearer and to offer a signpost to the way a sentence is to be read. But what if one perfectly punctuated sentence after another carries on for three or four pages with no break? Can you keep your concentration? Could you remember where you are after an interruption?

If punctuation is a signpost, paragraphing is a road map which should help you to find your way through a piece of writing.

There are no rules about the length of paragraphs. In some cases a very long paragraph may be necessary to put over a difficult point. In other cases a very short paragraph may work very well. If you're telling a story about being lost on the moors, a paragraph of three or four words ('The fog thickened' or, 'There was the village!') might stand out effectively.

Practice

In many cases it is useful to begin a paragraph with a **topic sentence** (less important in stories). This tells the reader what the paragraph is about.

If you are writing about the character of Macbeth, or perhaps giving your opinion on animal welfare, starting with sentences like this helps:

Macbeth is troubled by his guilt throughout the play.

(A paragraph referring to examples from his first murder up to the end of the play.)

Many people feel sympathy for animals, but still help to cause their deaths.

(A paragraph about food, cosmetic testing, leather handbags, etc.)

There are many pressures today which work against school sport.

(A paragraph bringing in examples from selling off playing fields to demands on teachers'/pupils' time)

Short paragraphs 1

Read the following one-sentence paragraphs and think of a situation in a fictional story where they could work really well. This is just a chance to use your imagination:
- 'My name is Bruce Reid,' he said.
- The road stretched ahead, miles of emptiness.
- The box was empty.
- It was the border.
- There could be no doubt – the sock was certainly blue.

You'll find some suggestions on the next page.

Paragraphing speech

There are two useful rules concerning paragraphing speech.
- In most cases you should make a new line when a new speech starts. This makes things clearer for the reader. Also, when there is a conversation between two or more people, you can leave out the boring repeats of 'George said …' and 'Maria replied …'
- A very long speech may have several paragraphs. If so, re-open the speech marks for each paragraph, but don't close them until the end of the speech. If you close speech marks and re-open them for the next paragraph, that means there is a new speaker.

43

Short paragraphs 2

Some of the single-sentence paragraphs suggest a storyline quite clearly, such as the lost traveller stranded in a desert, the discovery of a robbery (though it could be a lost letter or a missing weapon), the prisoners of war or persecuted citizens reaching freedom. How about the top one? It seems quite innocent, but not if you've been pursued by a mystery man or there's news of a dangerous criminal (Bruce Reid) on the loose. The last one reminds us that you can use the short paragraph for a humorous shock as well as a dramatic one: have you just done an important interview in odd socks?

Indicate your paragraphs clearly

Traditionally the rule was to **indent** at the start of a paragraph (this means start a few spaces in from the margin). You can still do this if you want, but it's now more common to leave a line space between paragraphs. What you must do is make clear where a new paragraph starts. If there's a full line of print on the line before, it can be confusing unless you line-space or indent.

Try it yourself!

Feeling at home with paragraphs

It's not possible to test your knowledge of paragraphs in the same way as other features of language. Paragraphs are too long for short tests and it's not so easy to mark right or wrong.

So instead, here are three writing exercises. Try to get used to the idea of a paragraph as something that fits together as a unit. When writing about books or writing a factual piece, it's useful to plan by thinking, 'Then I'll have a paragraph about …'

1 Choose one of the topic sentences on **page 43** and write the paragraph that follows. Paragraphs can be any length, but in a formal piece of writing like this, try to write something between six and eight sentences. Remember that using paragraphs and topic sentences should give your writing form and control, so try to connect ideas in an orderly way.

2 Write a piece of dialogue between two or more people. You don't need to write long speeches. Try to write it with as few speaker identifications ('Eric said …') as you can. Use paragraphing and punctuation to make clear who is speaking.

3 Write a descriptive piece about a person in danger and see what use you can make of single-sentence paragraphs. Remember that using short paragraphs all the time is not normally the best way to create drama. Try to create contrasts and sudden surprises.

Teacher's tips

Take note of how writers use paragraphs in your reading: novels, newspapers, magazines, non-fiction books including subject textbooks. Remember, it is about your judgement. Change of idea or topic? It probably means you need a new paragraph. If you have written a whole page without a new paragraph, look back – you may need to think again!

Answers

FIND THE SENTENCES (PAGE 4)

S (Sangeeta and Kate/went), NS, NS, S (I/will see), Q (the boy/did bring), Q (the referee/could see), NS, C (no subject/pass), S (digging the garden/tired), C (no subject/say), S (I/want), NS, Q (you/did wake), NS, S (to get all the answers right/is)

PUT THEM TOGETHER (PAGE 6)

You may find more than this, but here are some examples of sentences which can be reversed:
The new tram outperformed the bus. The bus outperformed the new tram.
The mayor praised the architect. The architect praised the mayor.
My brother knew the mayor. The mayor knew my brother.
You followed my brother. My brother followed you.
Sentences with both direct and indirect objects include:
The hunter gave the lion a chance (and other similar ones including: I gave him a chance)
The mayor gave him a medal.
The mayor paid the architect his fee.
The late goal gave my brother a medal.
The mayor awarded my brother a medal.

WATCH OUT FOR PRONOUNS (PAGE 6)

them; her; I; me; she, me, her

CHOOSE YOUR COMPLEMENT (PAGE 8)

Here are some suggestions:

head of the company, extremely agitated, his proudest possession, made of oak, in the hall, happy, in the brochure, expensive, my first choice, boring, world champions, unbeatable, in England's group, the capital city, in the South, very busy

MIXING THE SENTENCES (PAGE 10)

Here are some suggestions:

Tony became happy.
The school offered the children a party.
Mr Shah seems in a temper in the garden.
Too late, Tony gave the children advice.
Every May, at five o'clock after work, Mr Shah generously gave the children a party in the park across the river.

FORMING COMPOUND SENTENCES (PAGE 12)

but, so, and, comma/and, or, so, but, or

IS THERE SOMETHING SHORTER? (PAGE 12)

Here are some suggestions:

With more beds the new hospital will serve the community more successfully.
You can buy much cheaper groceries at the new supermarket.
Having checked her mirrors, my mother pulled out into the traffic.

ALTER THE MEANING (PAGE 14)

because/as, although, unless, if/whenever

Here are some suggestions:

When (or *After*) the teacher asked me, I helped to collect in the books. (time)
Before the teacher asked me, I helped to collect in the books. (time, showing your character)
Although the teacher asked me, I helped to collect in the books. (contrast, suggests you don't like the teacher)
We had no hope of winning *unless/before/until* Jane was dropped from the team. (three ways of suggesting Jane is the weak link)
We had no hope of winning *when* Jane was dropped from the team. (time)
We had no hope of winning *while* Jane was dropped from the team. (time, suggesting Jane, the star player, will come back)
Although Jane was dropped from the team, we had no hope of winning. (complicated, suggesting Jane is the weak link, but the team's pretty bad too)
We were in trouble *before/when* Ben joined the expedition. (time)
Because Ben joined the expedition, we were in trouble. (reason)
We were in trouble *if/unless* Ben joined the expedition. (two different possibilities – is Ben any good?)
I applied to Mayfield School *where* Mrs Schofield was the head. (place)
I applied to Mayfield School *when/after/before* Mrs Schofield was the head. (various different times)
Although Mrs Schofield was the head, I applied to Mayfield School. (contrast, suggesting you don't like Mrs Schofield)

Note how your choice of subordinating conjunctions can reveal what you think about Jane, Ben and Mrs Schofield.

Answers

WHERE'S THE FULL STOP? (PAGE 16)

I caught the bus from school to the station. I had to walk the last mile home.

The concert was sold out well in advance. We had no chance of getting tickets.

Mrs Jackson could not decide between Malta and Cyprus. The travel agent recommended Malta.

Jamie was amazed when he arrived at the airport. His best friend was on the same flight.

Katie left her books at school. She said she couldn't do her homework.

FIT THEM TOGETHER (PAGE 18)

When the bell rang, Mrs Harrison rushed into the room carrying a pile of exercise books. She was obviously in a hurry because she never even noticed that half the class was missing. From where I was sitting I could see my book on top of the pile. There was no room on the shelf where she always puts our books, so I took them off her before she dropped them all.

WHERE DO YOU PUT THE FULL STOP? (PAGE 18)

If you turn left into the town centre, you pass the cinema. The car park is just opposite.

Sanjay moved to a new school in September. He is enjoying it, but he says there is too much homework.

Where the river bends there is an old boathouse. I will meet you there after you have visited your aunt. We can go fishing. (**or: I will meet you there. After you have visited your aunt, we can go fishing.**)

WHICH PUNCTUATION MARK? (PAGE 20)

Our flight is due to leave at 10 o'clock.
When is our flight due to leave?
Would you mind passing me the chocolates?
I wonder if you would pass me the chocolates.
I asked you if you would pass me the chocolates.
When does next term begin?
I wonder who will take us for English next term.

USING THE SEMICOLON (PAGE 22)

We all thought the school expedition would be fun, but the weather spoiled everything.

The first coach set off at 9 o'clock; the second one waited for the latecomers.

When we arrived at the hostel, the thunder and lightning started.

The evening's activities were cancelled. We found the rooms were very comfortable.

The building was on top of a hill, so we had a good view of the surrounding countryside.

There was a river valley below us; I could just see woodland on the far side.

We decided to make the best of it. This would be home for the next three days.

MATCHING UP THE STATEMENTS (PAGE 28)

This may not be a complete list: you may have thought of good answers that are not given here.

I found an old coin in the garden: it was over 100 years old.

I found an old coin in the garden; my friends looked for one, too.

The school bus was late again: there were miles of road works.

The school bus was late again; we all missed school assembly.

I always worried about my music lesson; I never practised enough. (*could be colon*)

We buy most things at the supermarket: food, clothes, household goods and even books.

We buy most things at the supermarket: it's always such good value.

We buy most things at the supermarket; we usually go down in the car.

The journey took three hours: there were miles of road works.

I decided to leave the orchestra: I never practised enough.

We organised a collection for charity: food, clothes, household goods and even books.

We organised a collection for charity; we all missed school assembly.

I tried to find a really good hiding place; my friends looked for one, too.

46

Answers

THE COMMAS GAME (PAGE 30)

In July last year, while the school was closed for ordinary lessons, the council decided to run courses in road safety, first aid, practical science and various sports. Not surprisingly, the course on football was very popular, over 50 people applying for 20 places. The organiser of the course, Mike Stratton, hoped some United players would help out, but the team was on a pre-season tour of Portugal. All those who took part received four hours a day coaching, a snack lunch, a football video and a certificate, presented on the final afternoon. While the road safety course was also full up, numbers on the other two, first aid and practical science, were disappointing.

WHERE ARE THE COMMAS? (PAGE 32)

When you start a piece of homework, it is important to make sure that you have everything you need: books, pens, paper and, if necessary, a calculator. You should decide when is the best time to start work. If you have younger brothers and sisters, it is a good idea to choose a time when they are out playing, visiting friends or doing their own work. You do not want to be interrupted by your sister saying, 'Come on, Kirsty, have a look at this on television.' Your concentration on your work, even if you are doing something exciting like English, can suffer, but you must try not to be distracted.

Finally, you have everything you need and the house is really quiet. You open your textbook, find the right page, check the question you have to answer and make a start. For the next hour, except for when you get a drink from the kitchen, you are hard at work.

APOSTROPHES FOR LETTERS (PAGE 36)

It's been very cold today.
If I'm lucky, I'll get to the match.
She didn't call after all.
Claire won't change her mind.
He's willing to play if Aneeta can't.

APOSTROPHES MEAN BELONGING (PAGE 36)

Sarah's mobile phone, five miles to go, cauliflowers for sale, the school's reputation, fish and chips, passengers this way, the group's leader, my friend's name
women's rights, Charles Dickens' novels, both boats' oars, two pounds' worth, a girls' school, children's books

PLACE THE SPEECH MARKS (PAGE 38)

Anthony moaned, 'Tomorrow I've got to stay in and tidy my bedroom.'
'It could be worse,' replied his sister, 'you might have had to cut the grass.'
'They asked me,' said Anthony, 'but I said, "You can't be serious!".'
His sister told him to be quiet and stop making such a fuss.

SPLIT IN THE MIDDLE (PAGE 40)

'When you get back from holiday,' I said, 'come round and see me.'
'If you're so keen on football,' I said, 'why don't you come to the match tomorrow?'
'The train was held up at Dunbar,' I said. 'That's why I'm so late.'
'He's managed to lose his watch again,' I said. 'He's so silly!'
'I never expected to be back in time,' I said, 'but the road was really clear.'

WHO SAID THAT? (PAGE 40)

In the first example, the Chair of Governors says everything; it's all one speech as the speech marks don't close at the end of the first paragraph.

In the second example, the speech marks close at the end of the first paragraph, so the comment about the gymnasium and the classroom block is made by someone else (another governor?).

Answers

A FINAL TEST (PAGE 42)

When we arrived at the station, we all felt rather confused: the timetable said the London train left from Platform 2, but the departure board said Platform 5. *(possible speech marks for 'Platform 5')*

'What shall we do?' said Tony.

'There's no need to worry yet,' Anne replied. 'The train's not due to leave for ten minutes.'

I decided to see if I could buy a magazine for the journey. I wasn't sure if I had time, but Anne said the bookstall was just round the corner. While I went to get a magazine, the others decided to try to find someone to help us. The result was that, when I came back with my copy of *Heat*, they were nowhere to be seen. What a predicament! There I was, standing in the station entrance with no idea where my friends were or what platform the train went from – and now there were only five minutes left! I raced towards Platform 5 in a state of panic, then, just as I caught sight of Anne and Tony, an announcement came over the loudspeaker.

'Owing to track repairs the 10.45 to London Euston is running late,' said the announcer, 'and will now depart from Platform 7 at approximately 11.05.'